The Oval

Souvenir Guidebook

This edition © 2018 Scala Arts &
Heritage Publishers Ltd

Text © 2018 Kennington Oval Ltd

First published in 2018 by
Scala Arts & Heritage Publishers Ltd
10 Lion Yard, Tremadoc Road
London SW4 7NQ
www.scalapublishers.com
in association with Kennington Oval Ltd
The Kia Oval, London SE11 5SS
www.kiaoval.com

Printed and bound in Spain

ISBN: 978-1-78551-171-4

10 9 8 7 6 5 4 3 2 1

Text by Richard Spiller
Design by James Alexander
at Jade Design
Project editor: Oliver Craske

All images © Getty Images except
as follows:
Photo by Ian Marriott-Smith
Photography: flaps, 2–3, 7, 8 (top),
10, 25, 31, 32, 36–38, 40, 41, 50, 51.
Kennington Oval Ltd: 28, 30, 56, 57, 64.

Page 1: The pavilion in full splendour
as Pakistan bat against England in the
Oval Test match, 12 August 2016.
This page: The Oval in 2015.

Contents

Foreword by Alec Stewart

Opposite: Alec Stewart avoids a bouncer from Wasim Akram of Pakistan during the 1996 Test at The Oval.

Below: Alec Stewart celebrates England's win in the final match of his career, the Oval Test against South Africa in 2003, along with Martin Bicknell, Ed Smith, Steve Harmison, Andrew Flintoff, Graham Thorpe and Michael Vaughan.

For over 50 years I have been lucky enough to be able to call The Oval my second home. It was my home ground for 23 years as a player for Surrey and it also played a huge part in my international cricketing career. I played twelve Test matches and ten One-Day Internationals here. The century I scored in a Texaco Trophy ODI against Pakistan in 1992 remains a very special memory.

The Oval is one of sport's most iconic venues. Not only can the story of modern day cricket be told through its rich history but in the early days it also hosted a wealth of blue-riband sporting events such as the first FA Cup Final and England football and rugby's first home fixtures.

We have been privileged to have witnessed some of cricket's most iconic matches featuring some of the sport's greatest heroes. From Grace, Bradman and Hobbs to Botham and Kohli, a wealth of cricket's legends have helped to write The Oval's unique story.

This fascinating guide will give you an insight into the history of this grand venue and how we are looking forward to the future.

The Oval and the Ashes

There is a good reason why urns adorn the Hobbs Gates: world cricket's most ancient battle, between England and Australia, is inextricably linked to The Oval.

The first touring side ever to visit England was an Australian Aboriginal side who arrived in 1868. They had opened their tour at The Oval in front of a crowd of 20,000. The ground then staged the inaugural Test Match in this country, in September 1880, three years after England and Australia had met for the first time in Melbourne. England, led by Lord Harris and including not just WG Grace but his two brothers as well, avenged their 45-run defeat down under with victory by five wickets. When Australia returned two years later and won an exciting encounter at The Oval by seven runs, the *Sporting Times* newspaper published a mock obituary of English cricket which concluded that: 'The body will be cremated and the ashes taken to Australia'. The Ashes legend had begun.

It wasn't until the following winter that an urn actually came into existence – Australia this time the losers, England captain Ivo Bligh being presented with the miniature prize by his hosts – but The Oval has been the scene for many of the most famous battles ever since, traditionally hosting the final match of each Ashes series in this country.

In 1902, Gilbert Jessop – 'The Croucher' – hammered 104 in 80 balls to earn England victory by one wicket. This became known as 'Jessop's Match', although it needed the last pair of Wilfred Rhodes and George Hirst to knock off the final 15 runs amid scenes of high tension.

While not every contest has been as thrilling as that one, some of the most memorable moments in sporting history

Opposite: England captain Michael Vaughan (left) raises the replica Ashes urn at The Oval after winning the great 2005 series. Alongside are Kevin Pietersen and Marcus Trescothick, who is holding the MCC Waterford Crystal Ashes Trophy.

Below: A pair of sculpted urns herald the entrance to the ground through the Hobbs Gates.

have taken place in Kennington. In 1926 England recaptured the Ashes for the first time since 1912, a period which took in the First World War. They won by 289 runs, aided by Surrey's Jack Hobbs (100) and Herbert Sutcliffe (161) adding 172 for the first wicket on a spiteful rain-affected pitch.

Don Bradman ensured Australia won on their next two visits to the ground with double-centuries, his 244 out of a mighty 701 bringing victory for the tourists by an eye-watering 562 runs in 1934. Yet even 'The Don', having already retained the urn in 1938 with his side leading 1-0, could only watch while 21-year-old Yorkshireman Len Hutton set a new Test record score by making an epic 364 in 770 minutes at the crease. England compiled an enormous 903-7 and Bradman was carried off after fracturing a bone in his ankle while having a rare bowl.

Above: The first Test Match in England was held at The Oval on 6–8 September 1880. Over 44,000 spectators watched England play Australia over the three days. Here England captain Lord Harris is seen fielding.

Left: The legend of the Ashes began with this 'obituary' of English cricket that was printed in the *Sporting Times* in 1882.

Opposite: Denis Compton and Bill Edrich make their way through a vast Oval crowd after hitting the winning runs to bring home the 1953 Ashes.

In Affectionate Remembrance

of

ENGLISH CRICKET,

Which Died at the Oval on

29th AUGUST, 1882,

Deeply Lamented by a Large Circle of Sorrowing Friends and Acquaintances.

R.I.P.

N.B.—The Body will be Cremated and the Ashes taken to Australia.

Ironically, Bradman's most famous innings at the ground was his shortest, ten years and another war later, with his side – dubbed the 'Invincibles' – already 3-0 up and heading for a fourth triumph. Needing just four runs to finish with a Test average of 100, applauded wildly to the crease and given three cheers by his opponents, he was bowled second ball by leg-spinner Eric Hollies to finish with his immortal career mark of 99.94. The door through which he emerged before heading down the pavilion steps for his brief farewell has now been named after the world's greatest batsman.

Hutton – a sculpture of whom adorns the entrance by the Edrich Gate – was captain in 1953 as England won the Ashes back for the first time since 1934, an eight-wicket triumph inside four days led by Surrey's spin twins Jim Laker and Tony Lock. When Denis Compton made the winning hit, a flood of emotion saw the crowd rush on to the outfield to celebrate yet another highlight of Queen Elizabeth II's coronation year.

There were marvellous moments of a different sort in the 1960s. Yorkshire's Fred Trueman made Test history in 1964 by becoming the first man to claim 300 wickets, while four years later England needed help from the crowd to mop up following a huge thunderstorm before Derek Underwood's 7-51 forced victory in the final moments of the match, squaring the series after Australia had already retained the urn.

Above: Donald Bradman after being bowled second ball for no score in his final Test innings, at The Oval in 1948.

Right: Fred Trueman relaxes in the pavilion in 1964 after dismissing four Australian batsmen to take his Test wickets tally to 301. He was the first cricketer to take 300 Test wickets.

Opposite: The doors through which Donald Bradman left the pavilion to play his last Test innings.

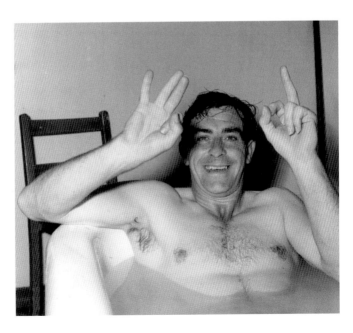

David Gower relished his own moment of glory as captain when his England side won by an innings and 94 runs to secure the 1985 series 3-1 as again the Ashes swapped hands. Although Australia dominated in the final years of the 20th century, they were still beaten in Kennington in 1993 and 1997. Steve Waugh's side was in no mood to suffer likewise in 2001, the hard-bitten skipper and his brother Mark both scoring centuries – as Ian and Greg Chappell had done on the ground in 1972 – in a total of 641-4. Only Mark Ramprakash's 133, on his adopted home ground, delayed the great leg-spinner Shane Warne for long as he claimed 11 wickets in an innings wipe-out.

Above: Champagne and beer flow as Mike Gatting, Ian Botham, David Gower (captain) and Paul Downton celebrate winning the 1985 Ashes on the pavilion balcony.

Left: England captain Alastair Cook kisses a replica Ashes urn after England win the 2015 Ashes.

Echoing Jessop's innings, Kevin Pietersen played one of the great innings in Oval history in 2005 as the hosts again fought to end another long stretch without the Ashes. England had surrendered them in 1989 and been heavily under the cosh in the seven series which followed it. They arrived at The Oval 2-1 up but their summer's work was still under threat on the final day until Pietersen's electrifying 158 caught the imagination of a generation to ensure a draw and launch massive celebrations.

Having surrendered the Ashes 18 months later in Australia, when they were thrashed 5-0, England had to win them back again in 2009 and duly did so with a 197-run success at The Oval, Australia failing to recover from being skittled in their first innings by Stuart Broad's 5-37. In the next two home series the Ashes had already been sewn up by England before the sides arrived at The Oval. In 2013, Alastair Cook's men were deprived of a fourth win in five matches only by bad light when just 21 runs short. Two years later Steve Smith's 143 enabled the Australians to inflict defeat by an innings and 46 runs. Arriving 3-1 down, Australia's 481 all out was met by a tame response from the hosts who were bowled out for 149 and 286.

Below: On the last day of the 2005 Ashes series Kevin Pietersen leaves the field after his innings that sealed England's series victory.

When The Oval celebrated its 100th Test Match in July 2017, England rose to the occasion. Their win over South Africa by 239 runs was sealed in the most dramatic way possible as Moeen Ali claimed a hat-trick. The off-spinner's huge appeal to have Morne Morkel LBW for his final wicket was initially turned down but the roar which greeted the overturned decision almost shook the ground.

Staging matches between the best players in the world is a monumental operation, requiring planning in the years and months up to the match, while each day requires up to 1,600 stewards, security staff, caterers and groundstaff.

While many of the great international moments at The Oval have involved Australia – not surprisingly given they were the opposition for the first 11 Tests, and they remain probably the biggest draw – many other countries have conspired to produce dramatic moments and landmarks in the history of the game. One-Day Internationals, including two Champions Trophy finals, and Twenty20 clashes have added to that harvest.

It was appropriate that South Africa should be the opponents for the 100th Test given they were the first non-antipodean opponents in 1907, when they claimed a draw despite CB Fry's century in England's first innings. Five years later they had rather less reason to celebrate when they were routed by 10 wickets and failed to reach 100 in either innings, SF Barnes showing his mastery of the seaming ball by claiming 13 wickets in the match including 8-29 in the second innings. They have generally been on the back foot in visits to the ground ever since, needing Bruce Mitchell's marathon seven-hour 189 to save them in 1947 after being set 451 to win.

Opposite: On 18 June 2017 The Oval hosted the Champions Trophy final between Pakistan and India.

Below: Moeen Ali celebrates taking a hat-trick to win the 100th Test at The Oval, England v South Africa, 2017.

South Africa's tours were halted when they were sent into isolation because of apartheid but when they ended a 29-year hiatus in 1994, it proved a painful return. Having taken a narrow lead after the first innings, the tourists were made to pay dearly for hitting tailender Devon Malcolm on the helmet. Whether the big fast bowler actually ever told them, 'You guys are history' is a subject for debate but he ensured his own niche in the records by devastating them with a fearsome display to claim 9-57, the best Test figures ever recorded at this ground. England cantered to an eight-wicket victory so quickly on the fourth afternoon that the spectators turned The Oval into a massive picnic site.

Devon Malcolm leads off the England team after taking nine wickets for 57 runs against South Africa in 1994, the best-ever Test figures at The Oval.

If the tourists thought they were going to avenge that nine years later, they were not alone after Herschelle Gibbs smashed 183 out of 484 to put South Africa in a seemingly impregnable position. England trumped that with ease though: Marcus Trescothick's 219 plus a fine 124 from Graham Thorpe on his comeback to Test cricket and Andrew Flintoff's 95 drove them to 604-9 declared. Martin Bicknell and Steve Harmison claimed four wickets apiece to knock over the tourists for 229 and set up a nine-wicket victory for an England side which featured four Surrey players – Mark Butcher, Thorpe, Bicknell and Alec Stewart in his final Test before retiring. The South Africans finally took their revenge on their 14th visit to the ground, in 2012. Hashim Amla's mammoth unbeaten 311 out of 627-2 declared wore down Andrew Strauss's men in a victory by an innings and 12 runs over the side at that time rated number one in the world.

West Indies made their Oval debut in 1928 and suffered defeat by an innings on their first two visits – yet it was a ground which became a home from home for them later on, cheered on by supporters who had come to live in England and settled in south London. In 1950 Len Hutton's unbeaten 202 could not prevent spinners Sonny Ramadhin and Alf Valentine wrapping up victory by an innings and 56 runs – plus the series 3-1. So began a sequence of exciting encounters over the following decades in which the sides took turns to enjoy some handsome victories.

Vivian Richards scored his career-best 291 in 1976 at the end of a baking summer which left the outfield all but bereft of grass, his side registering an awesome 687-8 declared. Dennis Amiss's brave double-century was in vain as Michael Holding defied a pitch with negligible pace and bounce to claim 14 wickets. Eight years later Clive Lloyd's men were back to complete a 5-0 'blackwash', while The Oval saw Richards bow out of Test cricket in 1991, his farewell marred a little as England won by five wickets. In 2000 fast bowler Curtly Ambrose was another to be applauded off the field for the final time at The Oval, but he was unable to save his side from a 158-run defeat which secured the Wisden Trophy for England

Supporters at the Oval Test in 1963, as West Indies beat England thanks to nine wickets by fast bowler Charlie Griffith and a hundred by Conrad Hunte.

for the first time since 1969. When they returned four years later it was Steve Harmison (6-46) dishing out the bruises in a 10-wicket trouncing which brought the home side their own clean sweep.

New Zealand were the next newcomers in 1931 and did not get the friendliest of introductions to The Oval, despatched by an innings and 26 runs inside three days after watching Herbert Sutcliffe, KS Duleepsinhji and Wally Hammond score centuries on the way to 416-4 declared and then being dismissed for 193 and 197. Split tours have meant the Kiwis have often missed out on visiting south London and in 1986 their visit was wrecked by rain. Even nature could not prevent Ian Botham dominating the match. Having been suspended for the first five Tests of the summer, he equalled what was then the record number of Test wickets – 355, held by Australian Dennis Lillee – with his first ball back, which Bruce Edgar edged to slip. He soon followed that by trapping Jeff Crowe to set a new record. Botham also had time to smash fast bowler Derek Stirling for 24 from one over when England batted, establishing another international best.

Bangladesh and Zimbabwe have yet to play a Test at The Oval but important landmarks in the histories of India, Pakistan and Sri Lanka have all taken place at The Oval. Although India's debut at the ground came in 1936, their fifth visit in 1971 was the one which really stood out. Leg-spinner

Viv Richards relaxes with a cold drink on the players' balcony after scoring his highest Test innings of 291 for West Indies against England in 1976.

Bhagwath Chandrasekhar's 6-38 destroyed Ray Illingworth's men, who had won the Ashes in Australia the previous winter but could not avert a four-wicket reverse in a match which saw an elephant paraded around the outfield on the fourth day. It was India's first Test victory in England and enough to win the series.

They nearly pulled off another remarkable victory eight years later, when they were set 438 to win by Mike Brearley. Thanks to Sunil Gavaskar's 221, India came incredibly close, finishing on 429-8 after a tense final hour. Gavaskar was on the receiving end in 1982, and painfully so. Fielding close to the bat, the Indian captain was struck by a powerful drive by Botham that broke his shin bone and saw him carried off. Botham also sent spectators running for cover as he hit four massive sixes in his career-best 208.

Pakistan's first win over England came at The Oval in 1954 – just six years after independence – when Fazal Mahmood's 12 wickets in the match gained an unlikely 24-run success. It made them the first side to win a match on their maiden tour to this country. Their first series win in England was secured in 1987 by arriving at The Oval 1-0 up and amassing 708, led by Javed Miandad's masterly 260. Mike Gatting and Botham were forced to bat out most of the final day to secure a draw. Other than two heavy defeats in the 1960s and the controversial forfeited Test in 2006, Pakistan have dominated matches at The Oval, and their 10-wicket success in 2016 ensured a 2-2 draw for Misbah-ul-Haq's doughty side.

Sri Lanka will never forget their solitary Test at The Oval in 1998, given it provided a first win on these shores. Against a side captained by Alec Stewart which had just beaten South Africa, they surprisingly inserted the hosts and saw them make 445. That looked less impressive after Sanath Jayasuriya (213) and Aravinda de Silva (152) dominated a reply of 591. Muttiah Muralitharan then followed up his 7-155 with an even more remarkable 9-65 in the second innings for 16 victims in the game, engineering a 10-wicket thumping.

One-Day Internationals began in the 1970s and West Indies were the first visitors in 1973, easing past a makeshift England side by eight wickets. The Caribbean side were roared on to a heavy victory over Australia in the first World Cup two years later, Roy Fredericks and Alvin Kallicharran cutting a formidable Australian pace attack to ribbons.

Ian Botham dismisses New Zealand's Jeff Crowe LBW to take his 356th Test wicket, breaking the world record, 21 August 1986.

Dinesh Karthik, Sachin Tendulkar and Rahul Dravid of India celebrate their Test series win against England, 13 August 2007.

The Oval staged the final of a world trophy for the first time in 2004. Although West Indies were no longer regarded as one of the world's leading sides, it did not stop them producing a remarkable upset to win the Champions Trophy. Thrashed by England in the Test series leading up to the tournament, they worked their way through to the climax of the competition, held on a damp late September day, restricting Michael Vaughan's hot favourites to 217 all out, which owed much to Marcus Trescothick's 104. When the reply slid to 147-8 with 16 overs left, there seemed only one winner. But with dusk closing in fast plus a steady drizzle, wicketkeeper Courtney Browne (35 not out) and Ian Bradshaw (34 not out) inched their way to victory by two wickets with seven balls remaining. Skipper Brian Lara scooped up the trophy and, when his men finally found their way off the outfield, led them into one of the nearby pubs to celebrate.

Among the other ODI highlights was Jimmy Anderson becoming the first England player to claim a hat-trick in the format, finishing off the Pakistan innings in 2003 by having Abdul Razzaq and Shoaib Akhtar caught and then bowling Mohammad Sami. Four years later Dimitri Mascarenhas gave the home side's innings a late surge by crashing India's Yuvraj Singh for five sixes in an over, although the final total of 316-6 still wasn't enough to save England from losing by two wickets in the final over.

The Oval's second Champions Trophy final, in 2017, also kicked up a surprise when Fakhar Zaman (114) inspired Pakistan – who had toppled England in the semi-final – to 338-4 before they rolled over India for 158.

T20 internationals came to The Oval in 2007 – four years after the first domestic tournament had started, in this country – and it was West Indies who once again were the first visitors, drawing a two-match series 1-1. Two years later, the ground hosted nine games in the format's first World Cup, the highlight for many being Chris Gayle lashing six sixes – including one

across Harleyford Road and into the playground of Archbishop Tenison's School – as he smote 88 in demolishing Australia.

Women's international cricket started in 1934–35, and when Australia's maiden tour of England took place in 1937 it included a match at The Oval which was drawn to leave the series level at 1-1. England's women had first been granted permission to use the ground in 1935, entertaining Rest of the World, and the following summer two women umpired a match together for the first time. The 1963 Ashes clash offered two breakthroughs: Mary Duggan's 101 not out was the first century scored against Australia, while Rachel Heyhoe-Flint became the first woman to hit a six in a Test Match on her way to a breezy 37.

On their way to becoming T20 world champions in 2009, England saw off Australia in the semi-final at The Oval by eight wickets with three balls to spare, thanks to Claire Taylor's superb 76 in tandem with Beth Morgan (46 not out).

The best players on the planet have been regular visitors to the ground for special matches too in recent times, Asia taking on Rest of the World in 2000 – which the latter won by 15 runs – while in 2005 an International XI defeated the Asia XI by six wickets, raising more than £1.1 million for victims of the Indian Ocean tsunami.

Above: Ramnaresh Sarwan and Brian Lara of West Indies revel in victory over England in the 2004 ICC Champions Trophy final.

Below: England's Beth Morgan and Clare Taylor celebrate winning the Women's World Twenty20 semi-final against Australia at The Oval on 19 June 2009.

Best Performances at The Oval

Ten highest innings in Oval Tests

364	L Hutton	England v Australia	1938
311*	HM Amla	South Africa v England	2012
291	IVA Richards	West Indies v England	1976
266	WH Ponsford	Australia v England	1934
260	Javed Miandad	Pakistan v England	1987
244	DG Bradman	Australia v England	1934
240	Zaheer Abbas	Pakistan v England	1974
235	IR Bell	England v India	2011
232	DG Bradman	Australia v England	1930
221	SM Gavaskar	India v England	1979

For other Test-playing countries

213	ST Jayasuriya	Sri Lanka v England	1998
119	JG Wright	New Zealand v England	1986

Ten best bowling performances in Oval Tests

9-57	DE Malcolm	England v South Africa	1994
9-65	M Muralitharan	Sri Lanka v England	1998
8-29	SF Barnes	England v South Africa	1912
8-65	H Trumble	Australia v England	1902
8-92	MA Holding	West Indies v England	1976
7-25	GR Hazlitt	Australia v England	1912
7-36	GA Lohmann	England v Australia	1886
7-36	MS Kasprowicz	Australia v England	1997
7-44	FR Spofforth	Australia v England	1882
7-46	FR Spofforth	Australia v England	1882

For other Test-playing countries

7-84	GA Faulkner	South Africa v England	1912
7-96	Abdul Qadir	Pakistan v England	1987
6-38	BS Chandrasekhar	India v England	1971
6-53	RJ Hadlee	New Zealand v England	1983

How The Oval Grew

G rowing fruit and vegetables rather than high-quality grass pitches fit for the world's best cricketers had been the priority at The Oval in the decade running up to 1845.

Not that the game was unknown in the area. The county of Surrey was acknowledged as one of the cradles of the game, and for a number of years matches had been a regular sight on both Kennington Common – where hangings were often staged too – and Walworth Common.

The county club's predecessor, the Montpelier Club, proved an able midwife. Having lost their ground in Walworth for building – a familiar refrain in more modern times – the club members approached the Otter family, who had taken out a lease on The Oval from the Duchy of Cornwall, owners of the land then and still to this day. That explains why all Surrey players bear the crest of the Prince of Wales, otherwise known as the Duke of Cornwall.

Ambitious plans for the site drawn up a decade earlier had not come to fruition and in 1845 it hosted only a moderately successful market garden, so the Montpelier approach proved welcome. A remarkable transition was effected between the signing of the lease in March 1845 and the start of cricket in May as contractor M Turtle – handily located nearby – transported 10,000 turfs from Tooting Common for a fee of £300.

Not having a home worthy of the name had been one of the main obstacles to the creation of a county club, but that was put right by two packed meetings at the Horns Tavern

OPENING OF THE SURREY CRICKET GROUND, KENNINGTON OVAL.

in Walworth on 22 August and 18 October, to the cheers and toasts of those assembled. Surrey were up and running but their tenancy of The Oval proved to be rocky in the early years, requiring the intervention of Prince Albert – consort to Queen Victoria – to quash a scheme of the Duchy's which would have seen the ground covered in houses.

Accommodation for the players, never mind those watching the action, was distinctly modest until a new pavilion was commissioned in 1858, with a large club room for members plus dressing rooms. The views of residents in the area were taken into account when it was located in the south-east corner of the ground.

The Oval was already well established as a venue for hosting top-class sport – be it Test Matches, major football games or rugby union internationals – by the time the modern pavilion came into being. As a condition of the new lease agreed in 1897, architects Muirhead & Baldwin of Manchester, who had designed Old Trafford's new headquarters, inspired a red-brick construction which, flanked by two complementary stands and the Surrey Tavern, was completed in a remarkable six months, in time for the 1898 season. The final bill, though, was double the committee's original budget of £14,000.

Long before that, an even more famous Oval landmark had been established – the gasholders to the east of the ground,

Workmen put the final touches to the new pavilion, circa 1897.

construction of which started in 1847. They were designed to power the growing number of homes and industries over a wide area of south and south-east London. The daddy of the collection – number one – dominates aerial pictures of The Oval. Although the five became four late in the 20th century, and all those remaining have been decommissioned, the iconic number one has been listed, and its presence is felt wherever in the ground you are located.

Beyond the pavilion – later augmented by a west wing – accommodation was spartan, crowds forced to stand or to sit on wooden benches and concrete steps as they surveyed the action over the massive playing area. The boundaries stretched across every inch of the turf, regardless of where the pitch was sited, rather than being brought in and marked with a rope as in more recent times.

One of the few places spectators could actually find some shelter from the elements was the Vauxhall Stand, which began life in 1923, the only drawback of sitting there being that it was a considerable distance further back from the square.

The biggest challenge for the ground came through matters which had nothing to do with cricket – the outbreak of world wars. In August 1914, The Oval was requisitioned immediately and Surrey were forced to play their final home games of the season at Lord's, which included Jack Hobbs's benefit match. It affected their form very little as, when the season was cut short because of the hostilities, the county were declared champions

by MCC for the first time since 1899. Surrey got their ground back soon and some fixtures, mainly involving the armed forces and for charity, were staged over the next four seasons.

During the Second World War a prisoner-of-war camp was built on the playing field.

The impact of the Second World War was to be far more serious. Once again, the authorities quickly took over the ground but this time stayed for the duration of the conflict. Initially it was used for searchlights to pick out German bombers, and the ground was hit on a number of occasions, albeit suffering far less damage than some areas of London in the Blitz. A far greater challenge came from the decision to build a prisoner-of-war camp on the playing area, designed to accommodate captured parachutists. Although the guests never arrived, The Oval was in such a poor state by the end of the war that there were fears it might take three years to repair the damage sufficiently for play to restart.

New groundsman Bert Lock had other ideas. Demobbed at the end of the war, he started work immediately, engaging work parties to help clear the ground – which involved nearly 1,000 concrete piles of two feet in depth plus huge bases for the huts which would have held PoWs, along with miles of barbed wire. Scouring Gravesend Marshes for suitable turf, he relaid the outfield and set about returning the square – pockmarked by weeds – to a stage fit to host first-class cricket. Building materials were in scant supply but The Oval, albeit battered and bruised, was miraculously ready for the 1946 season, celebrating the club's centenary a year late with a match between Surrey and an Old England XI. It was witnessed by King George VI, who made a donation to the restoration fund.

Like many major sports grounds in Great Britain, The Oval changed little between what was reconstructed after the Second World War and the start of the 1980s. In the Sixties a new Surrey Tavern was built, a typically utilitarian replacement for its more gracious Victorian predecessor, which had been designed in harmony with the pavilion. But an ambitious scheme in the early 1970s, which would have seen a tower block erected at the Vauxhall Stand, failed to get off the drawing board.

At one stage it seemed the club might uproot altogether and move to a site near Tolworth. But giving up a ground with so much history – never mind the right to host international games and with such good transport links – proved too much to lose. Instead the old backbreaking benches which tortured many a spectator were steadily superseded by new bucket seats from 1980, bringing much-needed splashes of colour to a hitherto grey arena. The perimeter wall, which had been patched up any number of times and was easily scaled by those either brave or athletic enough, was replaced by another enterprising scheme which included rehanging the Hobbs Gates so that from 1984 they faced further to the west and allowed large trucks to enter the ground more easily.

Alec Bedser of Surrey shakes hands with King George VI at The Oval, 1946. Alec's twin Eric is to his left. The King was shown pictures of the Bedser twins before meeting them so that he could tell the difference.

Surrey's growing financial strength, improved by becoming the first club to sell advance tickets for Tests by phone rather than making people queue up each day, plus more ambitious marketing, saw the first major breakthrough when the old Taverners Stand – much loved but rather shabby – was replaced in 1984 by the Laker Stand, which included corporate boxes and an executive restaurant.

Development was the key to making the old ground turn into an all-year round asset – yet The Oval's future once again was to come into doubt. A fire at Bradford City FC's Valley Parade football ground in 1985, which saw 56 spectators killed, meant sports stadiums with old wooden stands were on notice and the situation soon became critical for Surrey. Without the necessary safety certificate, internationals could no longer be played and the ground would slowly wither away.

For some time a scheme had been in the offing to build an indoor training facility at the Vauxhall End to be named after Surrey and England great Ken Barrington, with £4.8 million raised to that end. When a projected grant which would have meant work could start fell through, it was time for action and the Save The Oval Appeal made it possible. It was launched by Sir Len Hutton, who had scored that epic

For early television broadcasts from The Oval the cameras were sited on the flat roof of the West Stand.

The Committee Room was moved to its present location during the 1990s renovations of the pavilion. This space used to contain the away dressing room.

364 against Australia, and a brick sculpture of him was created at the ground's main entrance as a centrepiece of the scheme.

As soon as the 1988 season was over, the stately but dated Nets and West stands were demolished, their replacement finally providing the county with an indoor practice centre rather than having to beg and borrow from the likes of Lord's and the Bank of England Sports Club at Roehampton. Building work hit several hitches and had to be phased between seasons but, in July 1991, the Queen – at that time the club's patron, later handing over to the Prince of Wales – performed the official opening of the Bedser Stand, commemorating Surrey's famous twins. It incorporated the Ken Barrington Centre plus new dressing rooms, a media centre, corporate boxes, a bar for members with fine views over the ground and workshop facilities for the groundstaff, who had been accommodated by a caravan for many years.

Another crucial stream of revenue came when Surrey's headquarters got a new name – it became The Foster's Oval in 1988 as the Australian beer giant took an interest. Another company with roots down under, AMP, later took over as title sponsor and then handed the role on to insurance firm Brit. Latterly, the club's commercial partner has been Kia and the ground has become known as the Kia Oval.

Keeping up the pace of change, major work was required to restore the pavilion to prominence as it was now overshadowed by structures on both sides. The loss of the dressing rooms had created extra space but the Victorian building's foundations also badly needed strengthening. So once the 1992 season was

completed, a programme which stretched over more than two years saw the creation of a first-floor balcony instead of the much-loved but single-row 'shelf'. The Committee Room was swapped from the eastern to the western side and extended. The roof was also lifted, creating additional seats plus space for a new members' restaurant, which was instantly popular and provides one of world cricket's best places to eat while watching the game. Work was completed in time for Surrey's 150th birthday in 1995 and even if the county's cricket that year was dire, there was plenty of room for members to enjoy the surge of success which began in 1996 under a team led by Alec Stewart and Adam Hollioake.

The heart of the pavilion is the Long Room, built in 1898 and renovated during the works completed in 1995.

While one end of The Oval had been updated, almost beyond recognition, the other was badly in need of improvement. Siting the Barrington Centre at the Pavilion End had been an inspired move as it made room for a more radical solution. Next to the increasingly aged Vauxhall Stand was a block which included corporate boxes for big matches. The 'semi-permanent' structure had a life of 15 years when it was put up in 1988 and it was prone to creak rather worryingly when it was windy. Both were swept away in the winter of 2003–4 to provide space for the OCS Stand, a revolutionary building which included an iconic curved roof. To borrow the money needed for the £25 million cost, Surrey secured an unprecedented 15-year agreement which guaranteed Tests and One-Day Internationals.

Eating up a slice of the outfield, which meant the view from the Vauxhall End was no longer so distant, the new OCS Stand provided spectators with a superb perspective on the action, increased the capacity of the ground to more than 23,000, and provided conference and dining facilities which could be used all year round. The roof terrace offers a remarkable view and is popular with spectators.

The stand also had new homes for the media. The Brian Johnston Broadcasting Centre – which had been opened at the top of the pavilion in 1994 to commemorate the great Test Match Special commentator and all-round broadcaster – was moved and extended for TV and radio. Meanwhile the written press had a view from over the sightscreen, their gallery now named after legendary Wisden Cricketers' Almanack editor Sydney Pardon. Again constructed over two years around the fixture list, the OCS Stand was completed in time for the 2005 season and proved the perfect background as England won back the Ashes for the first time in 18 years.

Inevitably, not every project can be consummated yet the ground has continued to evolve. The Surrey Tavern was swept away in 2008, its pub long closed and banqueting suite now obsolete. It offered the opportunity for The Oval to present a much happier face to the many visitors making their way from Oval Tube Station, allowing the Hobbs Gates to be relocated

Below: Aerial view from the north during 2017. In the foreground is the OCS Stand with its 'living wall' of shrubs and plants.

Overleaf: A view of the OCS Stand under floodlights during the T20 Blast match between Surrey and Glamorgan on 4 August 2017.

Above: The Sydney Pardon Press Box, located within the OCS Stand.

Opposite: The pavilion's face to the outside world was remodelled in 2013 with the addition of the Galadari Terrace.

once more so that entry and exit would be much easier for spectators, particularly on major occasions. That process was completed in 2013 when the Galadari Terrace, replete with Doric columns and urns which signify the ground's Ashes history, was added to the pavilion.

Back in 1997, Surrey had been poised to host the inaugural day–night limited overs match in England, only for a deluge to flood the ground and the honour to pass to Edgbaston. Temporary lights had to be hauled on and off the ground until, in 2009, The Oval acquired its own permanent set. At the same time, massive winter work on the outfield finally swept away those turfs from Gravesend to bring a vastly improved drainage system, which pays back its investment with every season.

The old Mound Stand, updated and renamed after Tony Lock in 1984, was demolished three decades later, when the Laker Stand became the Lock & Laker Stand to celebrate the two spinners who did noble service for both Surrey and England in the 1950s. Appropriately, it stands next to the Peter May Stand – commemorating their team-mate and captain – which incorporates a garden from which fans can watch or relax as they choose. That £10 million development, which accommodates 6,300 spectators, was opened at the start of the 2016 season and pushed the capacity up to 25,500.

Surrey and the
Wider World

Walk around The Oval and you can feel the history of Surrey County Cricket Club.

It's not only the great players whose pictures gaze down from the walls of the pavilion and the perimeter wall, marking their achievements at international and domestic level. The county's most successful teams are in evidence too.

The ground is the headquarters for cricket in the whole county of Surrey, which takes in a massive chunk of south London too, given that the English game still sticks to the ancient county borders. The Surrey Cricket Foundation, which is a charitable body, supports communities, schools and clubs throughout the county with funding, expertise and coaching aimed at getting as many people to play the game as possible. The Foundation promotes health and well-being for all ages, particularly youngsters, and its agenda includes the strength of the recreational game and identification of young talent.

For those who rise through the county's coaching network, which leads into the Academy, there is the chance to join Surrey's professional staff and follow a tradition which has taken in the likes of Sir Jack Hobbs, Peter May, Sir Alec Bedser, Alec Stewart, Adam Hollioake and Tom Curran, plus overseas stars of the calibre of Sylvester Clarke, Saqlain Mushtaq and Kumar Sangakkara.

County cricket itself only became more organised in the second half of the 19th century and when the first semi-official competition was staged in 1864 it was Surrey who were hailed as winners. And although lean years were to follow, Surrey were commanding the summit again when the competition was formalised in 1890, John Shuter having assembled a side which had claimed or shared top spot in the previous three seasons. Under Shuter and his successor KJ Key, they were to be champions another five times in the following nine years as prolific run-getters like Bobby Abel – whose unbeaten 357 against Somerset remains the county's highest score – and Tom Hayward were matched with outstanding bowlers in Bill Lockwood, Tom Richardson and George Lohmann.

How the ground and the players who bestrode it have dominated the surrounding community is underlined by the way the blocks of neighbouring flats were named after cricketers, among them England captains WG Grace and AE Stoddart plus Surrey men Lohmann, Abel, Walter Read and influential president Lord Alverstone, who demanded at least three amateurs should be included in each game.

One of the features of Surrey's history, though, is that they have mixed intensive spells of success with long periods when trophies have been scarce. Other than a solitary title in 1914, when the climax of the Championship understandably took second billing to the outbreak of the First World War, there was no team success to toast in the first half of the 20th century despite the presence of master batsman Jack Hobbs, among many other fine players, and the brilliant tactical nous of captain Percy Fender over 11 campaigns.

Picking up after the Second World War was not made easy by the choice of skipper. Nigel Bennett had only played club cricket before the conflict but was surprisingly offered the

Opposite: Surrey's William Roller is still the only player to score a double century and take a hat-trick in the same match, which he achieved against Sussex at The Oval in 1885. This striking portrait of him going out to bat, by his brother George Roller, hangs in the pavilion.

Below: The team, members and officers of Surrey County Cricket Club pictured in 1911, in the painting by Charles H. Parker that hangs in the Long Room today.

captaincy in what appeared to be a case of mistaken identity, with his better qualified namesake Leo having apparently been the intended target. Poor Nigel, who had been a major in the war, could not translate his leadership skills on to the field, averaging just 16 with the bat, and Wisden Cricketers' Almanack stated baldly that 'want of knowledge on the field presented an unconquerable hindrance'. He wasn't invited back for a second season.

Surrey's breakthrough came in 1950, when they shared the title with Lancashire, but their developing team fully hit their stride when Stuart Surridge was appointed captain for the 1952 campaign, having told the club committee that his side would win the Championship for the next five seasons.

They did just that, the runs of May, David Fletcher, Ken Barrington, Tom Clark and Micky Stewart providing the perfect platform for a panzer division of bowlers spearheaded by a master of swing and seam in Alec Bedser and spinners Jim Laker and Tony Lock, backed up by razor-sharp fielding and catching. Two more titles were added under May to make it a glorious seven in a row.

Surridge's buccaneering tactics were never better demonstrated than in a victory over Worcestershire which wrapped up the 1954 title. Rain prevented the match starting until 2pm on the first day but the visitors were routed for 25, left-armer Lock claiming five wickets for two runs with the final eight wickets going down for just five. When Surrey

Surrey captain Stuart Surridge (far right) and his team celebrate beating Sussex at The Oval to win the County Championship for the fourth successive year, August 1955. Peter May stands at near left.

were cruising along comfortably in reply at 92-3, they were astonished to find their captain declaring but Surridge's faith in his bowlers was well placed, Worcestershire being bowled out for 40 this time and the game all over an hour into the second day.

Although the introduction of one-day cricket in the 1960s meant there were more competitions to win, Surrey went until 1971 before landing more silverware as Micky Stewart's side made a late sprint for the title. The Benson & Hedges Cup was added three years later, when they were led by prolific opener John Edrich, but it would be another eight years until they tasted victory again, making up for losing three finals in a row by thrashing Warwickshire in the 1982 NatWest Trophy final.

Eventually famine turned back to feast again at the close of the 20th century. Winning the Sunday League in 1996 lit the fuse and opened a glorious era. Under the stirring leadership of Adam Hollioake – his key bowlers the homegrown swing champion Martin Bicknell and Pakistani off-spinner Saqlain Mushtaq – the County Championship was won three times between 1999 and 2002, the Benson & Hedges twice (1997 and

Cricket fever in the local community: boys peer over the wall at The Oval during the 1956 Ashes Test.

2001) and a second Sunday success in 2003 was augmented by the inaugural Twenty20 Cup. Just as in the 1950s, Surrey managed to dominate the domestic scene while still providing a healthy contingent of players to the national side, with England regulars Alec Stewart, Graham Thorpe and Mark Butcher joined on a more occasional basis by Bicknell, Adam and Ben Hollioake, Alistair Brown, Ian Ward, Ian Salisbury and Alex Tudor.

Like their predecessors, though, once that side faded away it became harder to sustain success, with the added complication of the Championship now being split in two. Surrey were relegated three times but bounced back on each occasion, rebuilding with a combination of players developed through their own academy plus recruits from elsewhere and overseas signings. Their only trophy came in the CB40 Trophy at Lord's in 2011 but they reached three successive Royal London One-Day Cup finals between 2015 and 2017, only to be vanquished each time.

The Kia Super League has offered a new platform for women's cricket in England and the Surrey Stars – featuring leading players like Natalie Sciver, Tammy Beaumont, Laura Marsh and South African Marizanne Kapp – have earned a loyal following. It was fitting that in 2015 the county appointed Lambeth-born Ebony-Jewel Rainford-Brent, who had risen through the county's ranks to international status, as their first director of women's cricket.

Where once Surrey had a distant relationship with their neighbours, much has changed since the building of the OCS

The Surrey team before the Benson & Hedges Cup semi-final against Nottinghamshire at The Oval, 2001. Back row: Keith Medlycott (coach), Nadeem Shahid, Ben Hollioake, Ed Giddins, Alex Tudor, Ian Salisbury, Ian Ward, John Gloster (physiotherapist). Front row: Saqlain Mushtaq, Mark Butcher, Adam Hollioake (captain), Alec Stewart, Martin Bicknell, Alistair Brown.

Natalie Sciver of Surrey Stars poses for a selfie during a Kia Super League match against Yorkshire Diamonds.

Stand in 2004–5, the living wall of shrubs and plants helping to protect the surrounding streets from noise on big occasions. A Stadium Monitoring Group, held quarterly, is a forum for residents, community leaders and representatives from Lambeth Council to raise any concerns and be kept abreast of developments.

The grassroots of the game might seem distant when The Oval is the stage for global events, but just across the road in Kennington Park is a ground with an artificial pitch and nets where local people can play and into which investment from the Foundation – and its predecessor the Surrey Cricket Board – has been made.

An increasing profile for disability cricket – Surrey were the first county to set up deaf teams at both senior and junior levels – sees squads training regularly, work with special needs schools allowing increased access for youngsters and an annual disability day at The Oval.

Having invested generously in new facilities at Guildford Cricket Club and the Surrey Cricket Centre at George Abbot School nearby in Burpham, the Foundation's work reaches right around the county's boundaries. Each school in the county is invited to a match once a year, free of charge, with some taking the chance to add a trip to the nearby Vauxhall City Farm, while the Ben Hollioake Learning Centre – commemorating the much-loved Surrey and England all-rounder whose life was tragically cut short at the age of 24 – offers extracurricular opportunities for more than 400 pupils per term from schools in south London.

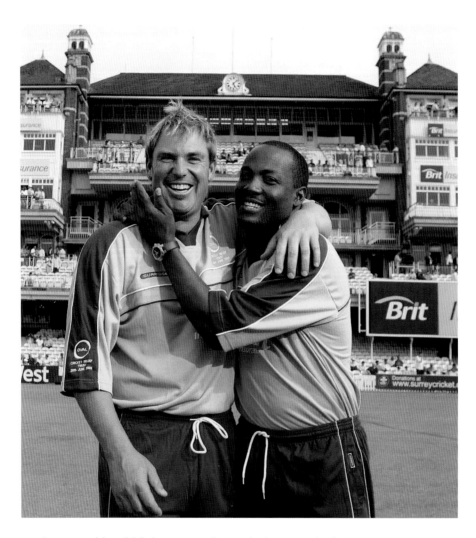

A partnership which has grown increasingly strong is the link with the Evelina London Children's Hospital, based at St Thomas's Hospital on the south side of Westminster Bridge. Surrey's players are heavily involved in raising money for a cause that supports families from ante-natal diagnosis through to childhood and adolescence.

The Oval turned blue on the Saturday of several Tests in support of Cricket United, bringing together the three main charities involved in cricket: Chance to Shine, the UK's largest sporting initiative which aims to grow the game in state schools; the Professional Cricketers' Association's benevolent fund, which assists former cricketers and their families who have hit on hard times; and the Lord's Taverners, who enhance the lives of disadvantaged and disabled young people through cricket and other forms of recreation.

Shane Warne and Brian Lara before the Asia XI vs International XI Tsunami Twenty20 relief match for The Oval Cricket Relief Trust in June 2005.

Surrey's reach took on global dimensions in the 21st century following two disasters. The Indian Ocean tsunami of December 2004 killed up to 280,000 people and one of the countries to suffer devastation was Sri Lanka. An appeal overseen by the International Cricket Council saw several matches staged round the world, one of them at The Oval the following June when Asia, captained by Rahul Dravid, met a Rest of the World side led by Brian Lara in a T20 encounter which drew a capacity crowd. A magnificent sum of £1 million was raised with the aid of Brit Insurance and devoted to rebuilding the shattered community of Maggona. Reconstruction of homes and community buildings was marked by streets bearing the names of Alec Stewart and Graham Thorpe while a new cricket ground built to first-class standard in nearby Seenigama celebrated the relationship.

The 1994 Rwanda genocide, in which approximately 800,000 men, women and children were slaughtered and many more fled, was behind Surrey's next overseas expedition. It was prompted by Alby Shale, who was determined to continue the efforts of his father Christopher, who had set up the Rwanda Cricket Stadium Foundation to help the east African country recover by building a new ground near Kigali. Christopher's death in 2011 stirred Alby to draw attention to the cause two years later by breaking the world record for the longest ever individual batting net. Offered the facilities in the Ken Barrington Centre, he kept going for more than 26 hours and Surrey were so impressed that they made the cause their next overseas charity partner. At the inaugural Cricket Builds Hope tournament to launch the ground in 2017, the Christopher Shale XI were sponsored by Surrey and proudly wore shirts bearing the Kia name and Prince of Wales feathers.

Legends of The Oval

Ken Barrington and the Bedser Twins

Ken Barrington formed the backbone of Surrey and England's batting through much of the 1950s and 1960s, a Test average of just under 60 testament to his stature. He was part of the Surrey side which won seven successive County Championships, and for county and country he often took on the unglamorous role of sheet anchor, forsaking his own ability to play all the shots. One Australian opponent reckoned that you could see the Union Jack trailing behind him.

His career was ended by one heart attack aged 38, but he went on to become an England selector and much-loved coach, and a father figure to young players, before he died of a second heart attack aged just 50 while assistant manager for England's 1981 tour of West Indies. His love of cricket and relish for coaching young players has its legacy today in the Ken Barrington Indoor Centre at The Oval.

The Bedser twins first joined Surrey in 1938 but almost immediately found their careers put on hold by the Second World War. When cricket resumed afterwards Alec Bedser quickly became the mainstay of England's attack, his Test debut being only his 13th first-class match, and his control of seam and swing relentlessly tested batsmen. He went on to play 51 Tests, taking what was then a record 236 wickets – often with little support – and claiming 1,924 first-class victims. Don Bradman rated him among his doughtiest opponents.

Eric Bedser's role in Surrey's glory years could easily be overlooked but his 14,716 runs and 833 wickets were a considerable contribution for an off-spinner who often had to take second billing behind Jim Laker. He might easily have been envious of his twin's success but instead was proud that

Opposite: Alec Bedser in 1950, when he was the undisputed leader of the England bowling attack.

Right: Ken Barrington in 1966. Having emerged through Surrey's all-conquering 1950s team, he became a formidable Test batsman.

June Mendoza's portrait of Alec and Eric Bedser that hangs in the Long Room. The twins are depicted in their Woking home but the imaginary view out of their window is of The Oval.

Alec went on to become chairman of the England selectors for 13 years and in 1997 was knighted. In 1991 the new stand at The Oval was named after them both.

Micky and Alec Stewart

Has any family contributed more to Surrey cricket than the Stewarts?

Micky, who played eight Tests for England, was a key member of the Surrey side which won seven County Championship titles in a row in the 1950s, vital not just for his batting but also his close catching – he claimed a world record seven catches in one innings at Northampton in 1957. A prolific run-scorer, with more than 26,000 in the first-class game, he captained Surrey for 10 seasons and led them to the Championship in 1971. And when the club's fortunes had waned badly, he returned as the first cricket manager at The Oval in 1979, leading a stirring revival.

That in turn led to becoming England's first boss in 1986, and he went on to be director of coaching for the ECB. He wasn't finished with Surrey, though, returning to be president and continuing to take an interest in the development of young players, his huge contribution resulting in the club's headquarters being renamed the Micky Stewart Members' Pavilion in 2017.

Son Alec has added yet more lustre to the Stewart name. His 133 Tests and 170 One-Day Internationals made him one of England's most capped players – and with 8,463 Test runs one of the most prolific. He opened the batting in pugnacious and prolific style and often kept wicket. He captained his country to victory over South Africa in 1998, when major series wins

were almost unknown, and led them in the 1998–99 Ashes and World Cup which followed.

Having been part of the Surrey side which dominated domestic cricket at the turn of the 21st century, he retired in 2003 but continued to be involved with the county, first as executive director and then director of cricket from 2013. The Alec Stewart Gate at the Vauxhall End marks his achievements and in true family style he reckoned: 'You can't get into the pavilion without going through a gate, can you?'

Sir Jack Hobbs and Peter May

Jack Hobbs is the only man in the history of cricket to pass 60,000 first-class runs. Joining Surrey in 1903, he became known as 'The Master' for his command of the crease, which was matched by innate modesty. Hobbs scored 197 centuries, more than half of them after the age of 40, and he formed prolific opening partnerships with Tom Hayward and Andy Sandham for Surrey and Herbert Sutcliffe for England. He played 61 Tests, averaging 56.

But for the First World War and another season out with appendicitis, Hobbs might have broken even more bowlers' hearts. Such was the esteem in which he was held that when he retired in 1934 Surrey inaugurated the Hobbs

Gates and they remain the main entrance to the ground. An even greater honour was bestowed when he became the first professional cricketer to be knighted in 1953.

Peter May, a dominant figure in the 1950s for both county and country, is regarded as England's finest post-war batsman. 'When he had that look in his eyes you just gave him the strike and enjoyed watching from the other end,' said one of his Surrey colleagues. A pupil at Charterhouse School in Godalming before heading to Cambridge University, May always seemed destined for great things and lived up to his billing in 66 Tests, 41 of them as England captain at a time they were the best team in the world.

May also took charge of Surrey after Stuart Surridge had led them to five successive County Championship titles, and added another two. His 85 first-class centuries could have been many more but for ill-health which cut short his career in 1963, at the age of 32. His contribution to cricket did not cease: he became an England selector for two periods, an ICC referee and president of both Surrey and MCC. The Peter May Stand is named in recognition of his huge contribution to the game.

Mark Ramprakash and Kumar Sangakkara

There were few better reasons to spend a day at The Oval in the opening decade of the 21st century than watching Mark Ramprakash bat. After switching from neighbours Middlesex in the spring of 2001, he dominated Surrey's batting through his prolific output and classical style. He scored 61 of his 114 first-class centuries for his adopted county before

Right: Kumar Sangakkara reaches his final first-class hundred, against Somerset at The Oval in September 2017. He went on to make 157.

Below: Mark Ramprakash after scoring 223 for Surrey against Middlesex at The Oval in 2010. He added 103 not out in the second innings.

he retired in 2012. While his 52 Tests for England – which included a century against Australia at The Oval in 2001, the first Surrey man to do that since John Edrich in 1968 – proved enigmatic, the county were lucky enough to see him in the triumphant autumn of his career.

In both 2006 and 2007 he averaged more than 100 in the County Championship – winning BBC's *Strictly Come Dancing* in between – on the way to becoming the 25th (and almost certainly final) man to score 100 first-class centuries.

If Kumar Sangakkara's time with Surrey was relatively short, lasting just three seasons, it was still spectacular. He joined the county as his magnificent international career with Sri Lanka was just ending, and eight centuries in 10 County Championship matches in 2017 thrilled cricket-watchers around the country as they took in one of the game's greats in action for the last time before he departed from the first-class game.

A remarkable 134 Tests, 397 One-Day Internationals and 53 T20s for his country, with 103 centuries in all formats, underlined his achievements, but the grace and precision with which he scored his runs and the influence he had over his fellow professionals – all over the world – were every bit as important. They ensured that he will always be included on the list of all-time world greats and among The Oval's favourite adopted sons.

Men on the Roller

It is nigh on impossible to please everyone but a very special group have been trying to do their best since The Oval was created – the groundsmen. From George Brockwell, who took charge in the early years, all the way through to Lee Fortis, who assumed office in 2012, they have faced a variety of challenges with the most important being the need to supply top-class pitches for the best players in the world.

For the likes of Sam Apted (who held the job from 1888 to 1912), there was the requirement to accommodate not just cricket each year but football as well, given that The Oval remained the venue for the FA Cup Final until 1892. Apted's determination to give himself the maximum possible time to get the square into shape resulted in brushes with the Surrey committee.

He was succeeded by his deputy, Tom Martin (1912–25), but it was the latter's brother, an imposing man known as 'Bosser', who rose to fame. His chief weapon was a massive heavy roller known as 'Bosser's Pet', and while the pitches he provided were the ideal stage for Jack Hobbs and his fellow

Bert Lock (right) was
head groundsman from
1945 to 1965.

batsmen to peel off centuries, they made the task of bowlers heartbreakingly difficult.

His retirement during the Second World War, when the ground was converted for use as a prisoner-of-war camp, left a mighty mission for Bert Lock when he started in 1945. Lock, who had played for the county before the war, also had the job of waking up the tracks and was accused by opposition teams of overdoing it when Surrey's bowlers were rampant in the 1950s, winning seven County Championships in a row under Stuart Surridge and then Peter May. His compelling defence was that Surrey were every bit as effective away from home.

Among the challenges for Ted Warn (1965–75) was protecting his square from possible attacks in 1970, when the South Africans were due to tour and there were fears of vandalism aimed at halting the series. Barbed wire, not seen at The Oval since 1945, was installed and had to be removed from around the square whenever the groundstaff wanted to work.

When Harry Brind arrived from Chelmsford to succeed the veteran Warn in 1975, he was faced with clapped-out equipment – Surrey's parlous financial situation had meant there was precious little money for replacements – and tired pitches on which entertaining cricket was almost impossible. A man who knew how to get his way, Brind persuaded the club to provide the tools for the job and relay the entire square. Experimenting with one pitch first, he dug down 18 inches and found there was little if any proper subsoil – foundation – so he used connections in Essex to install clay which had been extracted during the construction of the M11. Pitches at The Oval went from being among the slowest in the world to the fastest, and few visiting batsmen looked forward to playing when the West Indian speedster Sylvester Clarke was leading Surrey's attack in the 1980s.

Brind was also responsible for ensuring that his groundstaff concentrated on maintaining the square and outfield rather than sundry other tasks, such as cleaning the stands after matches. From Australia he imported the first 'whale', a machine which picked up standing water – later superseded by supersoppers and the like. His expertise earned him the role of inspector of pitches for the Test and County Cricket Board, which saw him travel both the country and the world, offering advice and support to his fellow craftsmen. He received the MBE at the end of his illustrious career.

Brind's son Paul took over in 1995. Like his father, he claimed the groundsman-of-the-year award for the best surfaces in the country, and when he left eight years later he shared it with successor Bill Gordon, who went on to monopolise the prize over the following seasons. Gordon had joined the groundstaff under Bert Lock in 1964 and was responsible for ensuring that there was always at least one cat in evidence at the ground. Chairs in the workshop were often occupied by felines when they weren't chasing mice, taking in some sun or snatching a glance at the cricket. Several were given the great honour of being buried on the outfield.

Such was Gordon's affiliation with The Oval that he became the only non-player ever to receive a county cap. He took over as the librarian and archivist while first Scott Patterson and then Fortis made their own contributions to a remarkable line of men.

Bill Gordon with his county cap. He was the first non-player ever to be capped by Surrey.

The Oval: An All-Rounder

In the decade before Australia arrived for the first Ashes Test in England, The Oval was already hosting international sport.

Cricket grounds in England have always faced the challenge of how to generate income beyond the season and Surrey were already feeling the strain by 1870. The secretary, William Burrup, hit upon the idea of staging a football match between England and Scotland – the first time the sides had met, producing a 1-1 draw on 5 March – but it was his successor, Charles Alcock, who developed the idea.

Alcock was well placed, given that he was also secretary of the Football Association. The Oval not only became the national team's regular home until 1889 but also hosted the first-ever FA Cup Final in 1872, a crowd of just 2,000 witnessing Wanderers overcome Royal Engineers 1-0. The military side were to reach each of the first three finals and it was only in the last that they finally enjoyed success by seeing off Old Etonians 2-0 in a replay. Until 1892 every FA Cup Final bar one was to be played in Kennington.

Rugby union also made its debut at the ground in 1872 and seven full internationals – against Scotland or Ireland – were played here by England up to 1879. With most of the revenue from football cup finals being taken by the FA, Surrey's committee decided in 1893 that they were not worth the damage done to the playing surface, much to the relief of groundsman Sam Apted. Rugby continued, however, to make sporadic appearances until just after the Second World War.

Cycle racing proved highly popular for spectators up to the First World War, the Surrey Bicycle Club and South London

Opposite: In November 2012 the first FA Cup Final was re-enacted at The Oval. This time Royal Engineers beat Wanderers 7-1.

Right: Charles Alcock (right), secretary of both Surrey County Cricket Club and the Football Association, with WG Grace.

Harriers staging regular meetings at the ground, which took nowhere near as much toll on the outfield as ball games.

Several other sports have made sporadic appearances at The Oval. Alcock's entrepreneurial spirit saw him embrace both hockey and lacrosse, which remained irregular visitors all the way into the 1980s, while baseball has made occasional visits – the first as early as 1889 – and could yet be back. An attempt to build a track for greyhound racing also fell through in the 1930s, while hosting an ice rink proved short-lived, even though the ground can look stunning in the snow.

Apted's successor in the late 20th century, Harry Brind, was no fan of Australian Rules given that it involved playing right across his much-loved square. An isolated game had been played in 1972, with a giant mat covering the centre, and was

followed by more regular clashes from 1988 as The Oval was filled by exiled Aussies taking their opportunity to taste home life for an afternoon.

In 2011 The Oval became the temporary home for Chicago Bears when the American Football side visited the UK, with New England Patriots and Denver Broncos also making the most of the facilities on offer for practice and media engagements.

But it is not just sport which has kept the ground alive in difficult times. When Surrey were struggling to stay afloat in the early 1970s, secretary Geoffrey Howard arranged a series of bonfire nights, Sunday markets, donkey derbies and funfairs. Football even returned for a while as the ground became the temporary home of amateur side Corinthian Casuals.

A far more radical idea was to stage a rock concert and on 18 September 1971 the ground, filled by around 40,000 music lovers, rocked to the sound of The Who and The Faces, led by Rod Stewart, on a stage built into the Vauxhall Stand. The gig was designed to raise money for Bangladesh, which had been riven by both a typhoon and its independence struggle. Two more concerts took place in 1972 with the likes of Frank Zappa, Genesis and Emerson Lake & Palmer performing, both again proving profitable, but new local authority rules limiting numbers following an incident just up the road at Crystal Palace made future events unviable.

Today many of Surrey's non-cricket activities are based in the OCS Stand, where corporate events, dinners and conferences bring a steady stream of visitors into the ground throughout the year. It was also the venue for the inquest into the Stockwell shooting over three months of 2008.

The Oval has been used as a filming location too, most notably in the 1953 film *The Final Test* which starred Jack Warner as a leading player making his final appearance for England. Fleeting appearances from contemporary internationals Len Hutton, Denis Compton, Alec Bedser, Godfrey Evans, Jim Laker and Cyril Washbrook could not rescue a leaden drama.

Fans of 1970s cop series *The Sweeney* were treated to a short scene shot in the Long Room in a 1975 episode 'Golden Boy', while in 2012 Hollywood star Tom Cruise made it onto the outfield but only so that he could land in one helicopter, change into costume and then take off in another while making *Edge of Tomorrow*.

A crowd of 40,000 attend the fundraising concert for Bangladesh on 18 September 1971.

2020 and the Future

As The Oval heads towards its 200th birthday, the challenges of remaining one of the finest cricket grounds in the world become even greater.

Tests and County Championship matches were the sole fare until 1963 and county clubs depended for the vast majority of their income on spectators turning up. Sponsorship and commercial activity were barely pipedreams for most. Now the varying formats mean games last for anything from five days to 20 overs per side. With the new T20 competition being introduced in England from 2020 by the ECB, the shape of the summer schedule is likely to see further revolutionary changes.

Hard hats as well as hard-headed thinking will be necessary at The Oval but current chief executive Richard Gould maintains: 'We're a cricket ground, not a stadium, and we always keep that in mind.' Imaginative designs are vital if the capacity is to be increased from 25,500 towards Surrey's ambition of 40,000. The first stage will be to replace the Lock & Laker Stand, with the aim to start at the close of the 2019 season and to complete it in phases by 2021. Then the attention will move to the other side of the Micky Stewart Members' Pavilion, where another large project will succeed the current Bedser Stand and Ken Barrington Centre.

'We can't expand the size of The Oval, so everything has to be done in the space we have,' says Gould, adding: 'In partnership with the Duchy of Cornwall, our landlords, we want any new developments to be sympathetic to the ground, our history and surroundings and the environment.'

The market garden which existed in 1845 might be long gone but what replaced it continues to flourish.

Artist's impression of The Oval's planned developments.